Things You Can Do To

HAVE A
FAITHFUL
PRAYER LIFE

ROBERT M. HILLER

CONCORDIA PUBLISHING HOUSE · SAINT LOUIS

1 2 3 4 5 6 7 8 9 10   22 21 20 19 18 17 16 15 14 13

Let's start with some good news: if you regularly attend worship services at your church, then you already have a faithful and regular prayer life.

However, I would guess that most people seeking a fulfilling prayer life are actually thinking about their personal prayer time. As Christians, we are a praying people. In fact, according to Peter, we are priests in God's kingdom (1 Peter 2:9)! When we were baptized, Jesus, our great High Priest who offered Himself for us, declared us to be priests! Lifting up prayers into the ears of our Father is one of the primary privileges and duties of a priest. So, when we want a faithful and regular prayer life, we are trying to figure out how to be more faithful in carrying out our priestly duties. How can we make time to pray? How can we be faithful in our prayers? How often should we pray? For whom or what should we pray? This book will offer the following five chapters on what you can do to get at the answers and develop a faithful, regular prayer life:

1. **You Can Go to Church:** A faithful and regular prayer life is built on the foundation of regular participation in the Divine Service.

2. **You Can Make Time:** Finding a regular time is necessary for a faithful and regular prayer life.

3. **You Can Prepare to Pray:** Going into our prayer time with a plan will help us focus our hearts and minds on Christ.

4. **You Can Pray God's Word:** Faithful prayers are prayers that are shaped and filled by God's Word.

5. **You Can Struggle:** Faithful and regular prayer lives do not come easy. The Gospel frees us to struggle as we seek to be more diligent in prayer.

Where do we begin developing a regular
and faithful prayer life? Faithful and regular prayer begins
with God. He comes to us first, and prayer is our response
to Him. God primarily comes to us as we gather for worship
to receive His Word and Sacraments. We call this the Divine
Service, because in this corporate worship God is serving us
with His gifts. It is critical for us to recognize the central role
of worship in our lives as Christians, especially its impact on
our personal prayer life.

I once joined a music club where I was offered a selec-
tion of CDs every month. I could choose which CDs I wanted
from their catalog, mail away my choices, and within just a
few days my CDs would arrive in the mailbox, ready for listening. Too often this is how we view prayer. We think up a
list of items we want God to send us, we mail off our requests
to heaven, and we await His miraculous answer to arrive in
the mail. We think we must take the initiative in prayer. Then,
once we've done our part, we just sit back and wait for God
to respond in a prompt fashion.

Prayer does not begin with our decision to approach
God with our requests. Rather, God makes the first move.
He stands at the door and knocks with His arms full of gifts
to give. His invitation evokes prayer from us. Before we
ever speak, He beckons us to approach Him. His call comes
in words of command and blessing, in words of Law and

Gospel. The Divine Service is the place where the conversation begins.

God's Initiative

Paul once said, "Faith comes from hearing, and hearing through the word of Christ" (Roman 10:17). This faith-giving message is both spoken to us and heard by us primarily when our churches gather for the Divine Service, where God approaches us in His Word and Sacraments. In the Divine Service, we hear God's condemnation of our sinfulness and His gracious call to repent. The saving message that those very sins have been graciously paid for by the bloody sacrifice of Jesus Christ is proclaimed into our ears and hearts. This Jesus who died for us has risen for us and now sits at God's right hand to reign over us! The sacrificial Lamb has become our gracious Lord who lives to forgive us, redeem us, guide us, and even pray for us! He comes to us in the Word that is preached into our ears. His true body and true blood are placed into our mouths for our forgiveness and our strength. By the power of the Holy Spirit, Christ gives Himself to us in the Divine Service and in this way faith is created and sustained in our hearts. This Jesus-wrought faith, then, is not silent, but very vocal in prayer. Prayer is the Holy Spirit-empowered voice of faith.

Rather than thinking of prayer as mailing our requests off to God, think of prayer like the results of a strong healthy rain on a dry garden. In the Divine Service, God has drenched our sin-parched hearts with His mercy, creating life where there was death, producing fruitful vines and branches where there was once only dirt. Prayer is the fruit that grows after the rain.

Without the Gospel-based view that prayer flows from God's gifts, prayer is reduced to placing orders to God. This is no better than the pagans who believe that if they constantly badger their deity, they will get it to do their bidding. But grounded in the Holy Spirit's gracious activity, prayer becomes a faith-filled conversation between the Father and His children. It's not a way for us to manipulate God to work for us but is instead a creation of God's gracious Word. In prayer we can trust He is hearing us and working all things for our good. We can rest, wrestle, rejoice, lament, sing, and weep, knowing that we are doing so into the ears of a God who will come to us again and again with promises of forgiveness, strength, and hope. We are praying to a God who promises to listen!

Prayer Comes through Hearing

What do prayers look like when they are spoken in response to God? To get at the answer, we must examine two questions:

1. What is God saying to me?

2. How do I respond?

To the first question, God has two things He wants to say—two ways of talking to us: He speaks to us in words of Law and Gospel. In the Divine Service, these words come to us in the liturgy and the sermon. As we will see, these two words will shape the content of our prayers (our response) both in the Divine Service and at home.

The Law is that word from God that tells us God's will. It tells us the expectations God has of His creatures. We Lutherans love to talk about what happens when the Law hits our ears. The first thing it does is keep us in line by showing the consequences that will come from breaking the rules, thus functioning as a deterrent from outward sin. Second, the Law always accuses us as sinners. When we compare our thoughts, words, and deeds with God's will, we see that we are sinners, and our guilt is revealed. Third, the Law guides us Christians to see what sort of life God raised us to live when we were born anew in Baptism.

Most often when we go to church, we experience the Law in its second and third sense. When the pastor preaches, for example, we either feel convicted by what he says or we listen for advice on how to live as baptized disciples. Thus, when God approaches us with His word of Law, our prayerful responses will be shaped by the recognition of our guilt or by our Spirit-wrought desire to follow God's will. Perhaps the following examples will help clarify.

THE LAW AND REPENTANT PRAYERS

When the Law performs its accusing work on us, we find ourselves praying prayers of repentance. Take a moment to read the account of King David and his murderous affair with

Bathsheba (2 Samuel 11:1–12:15). *Dateline: Mystery* couldn't have uncovered a seedier scandal! A hero king stays behind from his wartime duties only to get a soldier's wife pregnant. In an effort to cover his tracks, he brings the soldier home for some quality time with his wife. Unfortunately for David, the soldier has so much integrity that he refuses to enjoy the pleasures of married life while his band of brothers fights for the nation. The hero king, fearing exposure, fixes things with the commander to make sure the noble soldier fights on the front lines, thereby ensuring his death. The soldier dies and David thinks he is off the hook. No one was the wiser! No one, that is, except for God.

God sends His prophet Nathan to preach a sermon to David that utterly shatters his false security and exposes David's sin right to his face. David is undone, dead where he stands. He had broken so many commandments it was hard to keep track, and Nathan was there with God's Law to expose David. Standing before the accusations of God's Holy Law, David cries out, "I have sinned against the LORD" (12:13). Actually, we know that David had more to say than that. This whole experience produced one of the Bible's most profound prayers in Psalm 51.

When we hear of our sin, the proper response is not to get defensive and tell God He just doesn't understand. Rather, we are to recognize that God is right and with David cry, "I am guilty, and I need forgiveness." When we stand accused before our holy God, we are driven to repent. The Law produces such prayers of repentance inside of us because our consciences are terrified once we realize the depth of our sin.

At the very start of the Divine Service we hear the Invocation of the name of God, and we realize we are standing in the presence of our all-holy God and our lives have not been worthy of His glory. As we are confronted with our unholiness, we confess with the apostle John that "if we say we have no sin, we deceive ourselves, and the truth is not in us. If we confess our sins, [God] is faithful and just to forgive us our sins and cleanse us from all unrighteousness" (1 John 1:8–9; see also *LSB*, p. 151). At this point, confronted with our sinfulness, we join King David in crying, "I have sinned against the LORD." The Law drives us to repent.

THE LAW AND PRAYERS FOR GUIDANCE

Through His Law, God will relentlessly show us our guilt and, without ever backing off, show us our need for grace. Yet the Law is not *only* going to accuse us. In fact, for the baptized child of God (that is, for you) the Law is a great friend. It shows us how we are to carry out our lives as Christians. We have been saved by God's grace alone through faith alone only because of Christ's work on our behalf. Because of this, we are now able to carry out the callings God has prepared in advance for us to do (Ephesians 2:8–10)! However, when we see what God has called us to do, it can be incredibly overwhelming. We cannot and must not seek to carry out our callings on our own. We need help. We need guidance. Here, the

Law drives us to recognize our helplessness and our need for Christ.

David and Bathsheba's son, Solomon, was made king over Israel after David died. The responsibility to rule over God's people was too much for Solomon to bear and he knew it! When God appeared to Solomon in a dream and said, "Ask what I shall give you" (1 Kings 3:5), Solomon replied,

> And now, O Lord my God, You have made Your
> servant king in place of David my father, although
> I am but a little child. I do not know how to go out
> or come in. And Your servant is in the midst of
> Your people whom You have chosen, a great people,
> too many to be numbered or counted for multitude.
> Give Your servant therefore an understanding mind
> to govern Your people, that I may discern between
> good and evil, for who is able to govern this Your
> great people? (vv. 7–9)

Solomon recognized that he was helpless to carry out the great responsibilities placed upon him by God. It drove him to ask God for wisdom, but more than wisdom, for divine assistance in fulfilling God's will.

When I hear what God commands of me, I am inevitably faced with a responsibility that is too much for my weak and sinful heart. But God promises to hear my prayers and provide for my needs. When we have confessed our sins after hearing the Law in the Divine Service, we pray, "Forgive us, renew us, and lead us, so that we may delight in Your will and walk in Your ways to the glory of Your holy name" (*LSB*, p. 151). The Law will guide me, but I am too weak to follow. I then recognize with Paul that "when I am weak, then I am strong" (2 Corinthians 12:10). In my weakness the Spirit gives me what is necessary to follow the guidance of the Law.

As I write this chapter, we are anticipating the birth of our third child. Having two other children, I can confidently say with Solomon that I do not know how to "go out or come in" when it comes to being a parent. Still, God has called me to be the father in my home. This puts me right on my knees praying for God to help me, provide for me, and guide me as I seek to be a faithful father. "At least," I pray, "don't let me mess them up too badly!" As I walk into church on Sunday, all of my sins against my children come with me. So I pray God would both forgive them and give me the strength to do that which is too much for me to do perfectly.

No matter where God has placed us, we all need His divine assistance to do His will. Our relationships grow strained, yet God calls us to forgive and love. Our jobs become overwhelming, yet God calls us to be good employees or employers. Our parents drive us crazy, yet God calls us to not only honor them but also to serve and obey them. Our teachers make unrealistic demands, yet we are to work diligently out of respect for their authority. We find our prayers full of cries for help from God to do what we cannot do on our own.

THE GOSPEL MAKES PRAYING POSSIBLE

If all God gave us for prayers were commands and expectations, we would never be able to pray with any confidence. We would be too unsure of our worthiness to go before Him. Why would He ever listen to helpless sinners like us? How could David write Psalm 51 with any hope of God having mercy upon him? How could Solomon seek help in his calling with any confidence that God would answer in his favor? But both men pray with confidence, not because they were worthy in any way, but simply because they believed in the promises God had made to them!

In the opening verses of Psalm 51, David appeals to God's "steadfast love" and "abundant mercy" (v. 1). Concerning David, God had made this promise, "I will be to him a father, and he shall be to Me a son. When he commits iniquity, I will discipline him with the rod of men, with the stripes of the sons of men, but My steadfast love will not depart from him" (2 Samuel 7:14–15). When David sinned, he did so as one who had already received the promise of God's steadfast love. With such a promise, he was not freed to sin. But when he did sin, he was enabled to confidently cry out for forgiveness, trusting that God never goes back on His promises (1 Chronicles 17:25–26)!

Consider the prayer of Solomon again. He began by appealing to the promises God had made to David. He wasn't just crossing his fingers and hoping against hope that God would help him. He was trusting God's promises! Before his prayer of helplessness came this:

> You have shown great and steadfast love to Your
> servant David my father, because he walked before
> You in faithfulness, in righteousness, and in upright-
> ness of heart toward You. And You have kept for
> him this great and steadfast love and have given
> him a son to sit on his throne this day. (1 Kings 3:6)

As we saw earlier, Solomon's prayer revealed his inability to carry out the responsibilities that God had granted him. But Solomon believed in the promises of God's steadfast love towards David. He trusted that God would stay true to His word. God's steadfast love enabled Solomon, from his place of helplessness, to pray with confidence. God would help; He had promised.

Look at the Confession of Sins in the Divine Service (*LSB*, p. 151). The proclamation of the Law of God causes us to repent, "If we say we have no sin, we deceive ourselves, and the truth is not in us" (1 John 1:8). Though this realization may drive us to fear and cry out for help, it gives us no confidence that God will listen. But then the sweet promise fills our ears, "If we confess our sins, He is faithful and just to forgive us our sins and to cleanse us from all unrighteousness" (v. 9)! The promise gives us confidence that God will not only hear, but He will hear favorably. While the Law makes us realize our helplessness and our need to pray, the promises actually free us and enable us to pour out our hearts and open our lips!

Our confidence in the promise of forgiveness is then realized when the pastor, God's representative ambassador, proclaims in Christ's stead and by His command that we are forgiven. God has heard our cry, as He promised. He has been faithful and just to forgive us, as He promised, by sending Christ to pay the penalty for our sins on the cross. Our sins are given to Jesus who bleeds it away. Christ's perfect righteousness is given to us as we are now raised again to live a new life! It's a promise, sure and certain. Not only does such a promise free and enable us to pray, but it also produces prayers of praise and thanksgiving!

THE GOSPEL OPENS OUR LIPS IN SONG OF THANKS AND PRAISE

Thanksgiving doesn't just happen. We are not thankful "just because." Thankfulness is a response to having received something like a gift or to getting help when we are in a bind. Even then, we must learn to say "thank you," as it does not always come naturally. We are teaching our two-year-old son to say "thank you." We don't just walk up to him out of nowhere and say, "Hey! Say 'thank-you!' Now!" Rather, we teach him to say "thank-you" when he has received something from our hands. In the Divine Service we learn to say "thank-You" because the gifts we receive come straight from God's hands!

Our faith, which the Gospel has produced in our hearts, is expressed from our lips in prayers of praise and thanksgiving

(Psalm 51:14–15; Romans 10:10)! Faithful prayers regularly flow in the liturgy as the people of God gather around the Lamb on His throne. The constant flow of the Gospel produces a constant refrain of praise-filled prayers from the saints. For example, upon receiving the crucified and risen body and blood of Jesus in and with the bread and wine in the Lord's Supper, the forgiven saints sing a jubilant "Thank the Lord and sing His praise" (*LSB*, p. 164)! The Gospel produces prayers of praise and thanksgiving.

In many Lutheran churches, the Song of Simeon, or the Nunc Dimittis, is sung after the Lord's Supper (*LSB*, p. 165). Simeon was a man living in Jerusalem around the time of Jesus' birth. It had been revealed to him by the Holy Spirit that he would see the promised Messiah before his death. The day Joseph and Mary brought Jesus to be dedicated in the temple, Simeon was there. Seeing the fulfillment of God's promises to both Israel and himself, he cried out in praise,

> Lord, now You are letting Your servant depart in peace, according to Your word; for my eyes have seen Your salvation that You have prepared in the presence of all peoples, a light for revelation to the Gentiles, and for glory to Your people Israel. (Luke 2:29–32)

We sing the same song after receiving the Lord's Supper. Why? Because, just like Simeon, we have received the fulfillment of everything God has promised! We leave the altar singing prayers of praise because Christ has once again given us His body and blood to forgive us and renew us! Just like Simeon, we can depart in peace, confident that the Lord has gifted us with Himself once again.

The Divine Service and Personal Prayer Time

In a world of individualized spirituality, we tend to undermine the importance of worshiping with the Body of Christ. Yet the clearest picture we get of heaven here on earth is in the Divine Service. Heaven is not going to be a hallway of closets for us to frequent for private conversations with God. Rather, it will be more like a huge wedding feast! All the saints will be seated around the altar of the Lamb, singing, and praising our Lord for His glory! Thus, the prayers we pray and the songs we sing in church are most like the songs we'll sing and the praises we'll extend in heaven (Isaiah 25:6–9; Revelation 7:9–17)!

The gathering of the saints in the Divine Service is not a secondary activity that we make a part of our own personal spirituality. Rather, the Divine Service is the foundation upon which our personal spiritual life is built. Why? Because the Divine Service is where Christ has chosen to meet us. He comes to us in His Means of Grace: His Word and His Sacraments. In our personal prayer time, we are generally going to God with our prayers and petitions. But in worship, God is coming to us with gifts and promises!

As we go throughout our weeks, we are going to sin, struggle with friends and family, and have reasons to celebrate. Every day we will ask God for forgiveness and strength. We will give Him thanks when we experience blessings. Then we will bring all of that with us to the Divine Service, where we will hear what our Father in heaven has to say about it. We will hear God's voice in our pastors' mouths saying to us, "I therefore forgive you all your sins in the name of the Father and of the Son and of the Holy Spirit" (*LSB*, p. 151). And when we finally hear the sweet words of benediction, we will leave knowing that no matter what the world may do to us in the following week, our Father's face is smiling upon us and He is giving us His peace (*LSB*, p. 166).

Now, when I pray during my personal prayer time, I can do so with confidence. I know that when I confess my sins throughout the week, they are forgiven, because the words of the Absolution are ringing in my ears. My feelings of joy for the many blessings I receive are given a voice with the hymns I have sung. As the devil, the world, and my own flesh bear down on me, I cry out all the more faithfully to the God who blesses and keeps me in His mighty arms. A personal prayer life is critical. But without the Divine Service where God comes to us, our personal prayer time is reduced to the practicing of our own individualized religion.

By coming to you in the Divine Service, God has given you the foundation and model for a faithful and regular prayer life! When you gather with the saints in worship to confess your sins, rejoice in Christ's Absolution, intercede on behalf of others, and sing God's praises, you do so because God has given you a place and a time to receive His gifts! You can (and do) have a faithful and regular prayer life because when you come into His presence for worship, God opens up the floodgates of heaven and pours out His blessings upon you. Thus, a faithful and regular personal prayer time is founded upon a faithful and regular corporate prayer life.

Key Points

- God initiates prayer. Prayer is your response to the Word He has spoken to you.

- When God speaks His Law to you, you respond with prayers for forgiveness and help. Hearing God's Gospel message enables you to pray and to respond with praise and thanksgiving.

- Corporate worship serves as both the foundation and model of your personal prayer time.

Discussion Questions

1. Have you always understood worship to be mainly about what God gives, or have you considered worship to be something you give to God?

2. Which part of the worship service is the most meaningful for you? Why?

3. Do you consider corporate worship or your personal prayer time more valuable for your relationship with God? Why?

4. What are some ways you can take what happens in the Divine Service and apply it to your personal prayer time?

Action Steps

1. This Sunday, take notes during the sermon. Answer these questions:

    a. How did the pastor's sermon reveal my sin to me?

    b. What instructions did I receive?

    c. How did the pastor tell me Christ has dealt with this particular sin? OR, What has Christ done for me?

    Once you have your answers, take them with you to your personal devotion time and pray about them throughout the week. Ask the Lord to take what He gave you on Sunday and apply it to the other six days.

2. Take a hymnal or bulletin from your church to be used in your personal devotion time. Use the prayers or the songs to focus your thoughts. Make Sunday's readings the focus of your devotions. Try to make connections between what you heard in worship and what is happening throughout the week.

3. Find out the needs of your brothers and sisters in the congregation and include those in your daily prayers. Ask the pastor for a list of people to pray for or put your name on the prayer chain.

The title of this chapter is a bit misleading.

Technically speaking, you cannot *make* time. God has already made time. "And God separated the light from the darkness. God called the light Day, and the darkness He called Night. And there was evening and there was morning, the first day" (Genesis 1:4–5). Though we cannot make time, we are to be faithful stewards of the time God has given us. As human creatures we have been given dominion over God's creation. We are to tend to it and care for it. Time is an arena wherein we are able to carry out our duties. We are to give glory to God with the time we have been given.

Since time is not our own but is God's creation, we who live in time should realize that God, who commands us to pray, has given us the time to pray. You have enough time in the day to pray. Paul goes so far as to tell us to "pray without ceasing" (1 Thessalonians 5:17). Jesus often took time to be alone in prayer (Mark 6:46; Luke 5:16). We even see Jesus praying spontaneously throughout His ministry (Matthew 11:25–26). His time was full of prayer. Like our dear Lord, it is important for us to take time to pray. But that is easier said than done. If you are anything like me, finding time to pray is the biggest hindrance to having a faithful and regular prayer life. Too many demands and distractions get in the way of carving out time in my schedule. Many of the demands are unavoidable, necessary, and even good. But there are many other things that are unnecessary and a waste of time. With all of the demands being placed upon us, how can each of us best use our time to have a faithful and regular prayer life?

Time was made for us; we were not made for time. Calendars make excellent tools but terrible masters. In this chapter we will look at ways in which we can take control of our schedules so that we can regularly be in prayer with the Lord. A brief note before I begin: My hope in this chapter is to avoid legalism. That is, I don't want you to read this chapter thinking that God will be more pleased with your prayer life if you simply do what I say. Turning our prayer time into a legalistic requirement is a constant temptation. My intent is not to merely add another event to your day planner (though penciling prayer in won't hurt), but rather, I want you to see that you already have the time to pray and are free to do it!

Addition by Subtraction

How do you find time to pray? This is a practical question with a simple answer. To steal the old Nike slogan, "Just do it!" If you want to make prayer the main part of your day, then just make prayer the main part of your day. Easier said than done? Perhaps. But, remember, God has given us time, so there is time to pray. Often it is just a matter of finding time in our schedule.

The first step may be subtracting those things from our schedule that prevent us from praying and studying God's

Word and replacing them with a time of devotion. In fact, instead of merely adding prayer time to your schedule, why not center your schedule around prayer? Make sure that every day you have set aside however much time you find necessary to be alone with the Lord. Make it as much a part of your day as brushing your teeth or putting a shirt on. Once that time is established and fixed, you can begin to set up the rest of your schedule. Make prayer the priority by removing those things that are most distracting.

But what things should we remove? We all have busy schedules filled with important things to do: work, sports, school, family time, and more. It is going to be hard to cut any of these things out of our lives. So, is it even possible to make cuts in order to fit prayer in? Yes! But it might be challenging. At the risk of attacking an idol, I suggest cutting down on your time with technology.

Before you throw stones and smartphones at me, hear me out. Do you really need to watch TV? Is it necessary to check Facebook as often as you do? We have been convinced that we must be connected to some form of media. But why? Simply for the sake of being entertained? Being entertained is a good thing, that is, until it starts to dominate our lives—especially if we find ourselves spending more time watching and contemplating the latest reality show than immersing ourselves in God's Word.

You are free to turn off your television. You are free to shut down the computer. You are free to open your Bible and pray to God. You are free to sit in silence and process your day with the Lord. You can do it! We are addicted to noise, distraction, and entertainment. They have become lords over us. But Christ frees us from our addictions and gives us something worth focusing on: Himself!

We need to learn how to sit in silence and concentrate on the God who creates, redeems, and sustains us. We need to find ways to cope with the overwhelming world in which we live. Too often, we use media as a means of escape. It is easier to invest in a fictional character's problems when I know they will be resolved in thirty minutes than it is to sit and work through my seemingly unsolvable problems. It is not a sin to sit and laugh at your favorite sitcom every now and then. However, if we are using distractions and entertainment to cope with life's problems, we are not actually coping with life's problems. When the TV shuts off, our problems are still there. How much better, then, to shut off the distractions and cry out to the God who has overcome the world and promises to make all things right?

This is a matter of priorities. Rather than distracting yourself from the world with a few hours of TV every night, train yourself to present your concerns to the One who is Lord and can actually do something about your problems. If you are going to have a regular and faithful prayer life, it needs to take priority. You may need to sit down and analyze your schedule. What needs to be moved around or removed so that you are able to focus on God's Word and pray to Him?

Once prayer has been prioritized, it is important to ask the question, "When is the best time for me to pray?"

Finding the Best Time

Wouldn't it be nice to find half an hour to read Scripture and focus on prayer?

For many of us, even freeing up thirty minutes feels like a stretch. It seems almost miraculous to hear about monasteries that have up to seven points throughout the day for prayer and meditation. Finding time to pray is easy if you are a monk or nun living apart from the noise and mess of everyday life. Most of us don't have the luxury of exiting the world for prayer. Our lives are firmly fixed in the noise and mess! So where can we find the time?

It is best to set aside time where you are usually safe from the noise and the mess. For some this will be in the morning before the day begins. Others will find the evening, after everything has calmed down, to be a better time. Perhaps setting time aside at various points throughout the day will prove more fruitful. Everyone is different, and the Bible gives us no fixed law as to when to pray. Here are some considerations to make as you examine each of these options.

IN THE MORNING

First thing in the morning is an ideal time to pray. If, like me, you are not a morning person, you may need to set the coffee pot the night before. David affirms morning prayer in

Psalm 5 when he prays, "O LORD, in the morning You hear my voice; in the morning I prepare a sacrifice for You and watch" (v. 3). In the morning our minds are usually more fresh and clear. It is a marvelous time to bring our daily plans and concerns before God, seeking His blessing, guidance, and protection.

How are you to find time if your morning routine is already set? Simply wake up fifteen to thirty minutes earlier. Set your alarm a little bit earlier and use that extra time for reading the Bible and praying, or, as we have seen in the previous section, perhaps there are distractions you can cut out from your morning routine. Replace a few minutes of your favorite morning show with a psalm. It's that easy.

Martin Luther offers a morning prayer routine in the Small Catechism. When we rise, he suggests making the sign of the cross over ourselves while saying the triune name of God in order to remind ourselves that we are baptized (no matter what may come that day!). This is followed by repeating the Apostles' Creed and the Lord's Prayer. Of course, more prayers may be added, including Luther's morning prayer. I might also suggest reading a psalm or one of the texts from Sunday's worship service in order to give content to the prayers.

There is no better way to start your day than with prayer. Knowing that our dear Father has heard His baptized child speak into His ears sends us on our way confidently and joyfully. As Luther says, after we have prayed we can "go joyfully to work, singing a hymn, like that of the Ten Commandments, or what your devotion may suggest" (Small Catechism, Morning Prayer).

IN THE EVENING

Mornings can be difficult. As one who is not a morning person, I can attest that the snooze button is one of the greatest enemies of a disciplined morning prayer routine. Many people have to wake up so early that adding another fifteen minutes to the morning grind seems unreasonable. If you have very young children, you are likely fighting for every last wink of sleep you can get! For people like us, prayers in the evening may work better. Instead of finishing the day with some semi-tragic news story that likely has no bearing on your life, go to bed fifteen to thirty minutes earlier. Take the Bible with you to bed, read a chapter, and pray about your day. As David sang, "Let my prayer be counted as incense before You, and the lifting up of my hands as the evening sacrifice!" (Psalm 141:2).

Again, Luther is our teacher on how to conduct our evening prayers. Much like when we wake up, before you go to sleep, make the sign of the cross and say the triune name to remind yourself that you are baptized (no matter what has happened that day!). Follow this with the Apostles' Creed and Lord's Prayer. Other prayers and Scripture readings can be added. It may also prove helpful to learn a bedtime hymn to calm your spirit as you go to sleep (Small Catechism, Evening Prayer).

A word of warning about having your main prayer time right before bed: Though there is great benefit to reviewing the events of the day with the Lord, this can also be a hard time to concentrate. If you do not already have a regular pattern for prayer, evenings can prove to be a difficult time to focus your thoughts on God. This is especially true if you have trained your mind to be distracted and relaxed by the television. Shutting off the TV and starting to pray will require much discipline. However, this differs from person to person. I have had times in my life where I was able to concentrate better in the evening than in the morning. My parents always held our family devotions before bed, so my brain has been disciplined to pray before sleep. What matters here is that you find a time when you are best able to focus on your prayer and God's Word.

THROUGHOUT THE DAY

It may be that neither morning nor evening works for you. Prayer certainly does not need to be bound to such times. All time is God's, which frees us to pray ceaselessly! Though we are accustomed to spontaneous prayers through-out the day, we may also be able to find time to have focused devotions.

At your job you probably have lunch breaks or coffee breaks. Given the craziness of many homes, this may be the quietest time of your day. Take this time and use it for prayer. After all, you are in the midst of the very place God is using you for the good of His creation. Pray there for strength and wisdom to carry out your vocation faithfully!

My summer job throughout college and seminary was driving delivery trucks for a party-supply company. Very often, I was able to park my truck for lunch at a park and read the Bible and pray. Before I became a driver, I rode with a partner who would take extended breaks at his house. I was left to sit and wait in the truck. I used this time for studying the Scriptures and prayer.

The real danger with these kinds of prayers is that you have less control over your environment. I could never control when my partner would come back to the truck. Sometimes this meant cutting my devotional time short. If you are in a break room, you cannot control who comes in or goes out. You are also bound to be back to work by a certain time, which can be constraining and distracting. But if these are all things you can work around, then prayer at work can be a rich blessing.

Praying at fixed points throughout the day is a great discipline as well. I have heard of people who set an alarm to go off every hour so they stop to take a moment in the midst of what they are doing to pray to God. Before and after meals are also excellent for prayer. The Lord taught us to ask for daily bread. When we sit with our families around the dinner table, we are experiencing God's answer to that prayer. It is a marvelous time to give thanks, pray for each other, and even say the Lord's Prayer. Many of us have been brought up praying before meals. Luther suggests praying after meals as well (Small Catechism, Returning Thanks).

Ideally, the morning and the evening are the best time for prayers. But, unfortunately, that is not an option all the time. Whatever time works best for you is fine. Just make sure you build the rest of your schedule around that set time. Make that time sacred so it can be as free from interruptions as possible.

Spontaneous Prayer

I would like to give a few thoughts on the benefits and dangers of spontaneous prayer. By that, I mean those prayers we find ourselves firing up to God throughout the day. Spontaneous prayers are always found on the lips of God's children. In fact, when we find quick prayers on our lips throughout the day, we are keeping God's name holy! In dealing with the Second Commandment, Luther says, "Likewise, children should continue to cross themselves when anything monstrous or terrible is seen or heard. They can shout, 'Lord God, protect us!' 'Help, dear Lord Jesus!' and such. Also, if anyone meets with unexpected good fortune, however trivial, he says, 'God be praised and thanked!' or 'God has bestowed this on me!' " (Large Catechism I 74).

The *Treasury of Daily Prayer* (St. Louis: Concordia, 2008) has good information about structuring your prayer time. See the Introduction, pp. ix–xvi.

Who of us hasn't gone into an important meeting and sought the Lord's help by offering up a quick prayer? Or when you were in school, didn't you say a prayer so God would help you remember what you studied? When you see an accident on the highway, do you say a quick prayer for mercy and healing? When a friend is hurting, do you silently lift him or her up to God? Spontaneous prayers are evidence that the Holy Spirit is constantly directing our hearts towards our heavenly Father, "without ceasing" as Paul says (1 Thessalonians. 5:17).

In this sense, spontaneous prayers are marvelous. However, we must be cautious. If our prayer life consists of nothing more than random prayers throughout the day, then we will continue to feel dissatisfied with our prayer life. In fact, I would go so far as to say that if we do not strive for a consistent, set time of prayer, our spontaneous prayers are going to become fewer and farther between. Faithful, spontaneous prayers become the norm when our schedules are centered on an established prayer time.

If we reduce our prayer time to those times when our hearts spontaneously feel led to pray, we won't pray very much. If I only pay my bills when I feel like paying my bills, I will be receiving letters from collectors very soon. We have to be honest about our hearts because we are sinners learning what it means to be baptized. Since we do not always feel like praying, we need to train ourselves to pray at a set time or times throughout the day. Once we have disciplined ourselves with set prayer times, our spontaneous prayers will become richer.

I often hear that we should think about our prayer life like a workout regimen. If you want to be in shape and healthy, you are going to set aside significant time throughout the week to make sure you are training you body. You will become stronger and healthier. Moreover, this concentrated time of exercise will actually strengthen and enhance other activities you do throughout the day. You will have more energy at work. You will not get as winded walking up the stairs. Doctors' appointments will have more positive results. That time of intense exercise will impact the rest of your daily activities.

The relationship between a disciplined prayer time and spontaneous prayers works the same way. At least in my experience, when I have stayed disciplined with my prayer time, my spontaneous prayers become more frequent. When prayer is scheduled into my daily routine, I find myself thinking to pray more often in the various situations I face. When I am slacking off in my prayer time, I find that spontaneous prayers are less frequent. I do not think there is some great, mystical, spiritual truth here. Taking time to pray in a disciplined fashion produces spontaneous prayers.

We are God's creatures, bound to the time and space of God's creation. God has given us time as a gift to be used for His glory. When our dear Lord Jesus entered time, He used His time to pray. Even while dying for our sins, He prayed for our forgiveness when He cried, "Father, forgive them, for they know not what they do" (Luke 23:34)! Now that He has risen and is ascended back into eternity, He continually prays for His saints. "He always lives to make intercession for them" (Hebrews 7:25). When we take time to pray, we do so with and through the One who has saved us and prays for us eternally. There is no greater way to use your time than in prayer with Christ.

Key Points

- God has given you enough time to pray.

- It is important to prioritize your time and remove those things that get in the way of a consistent prayer time.

- It is important to figure out which time of day is best for you to pray.

- Having a regular time of prayer will make those spontaneous prayers more frequent.

Discussion Questions

1. What is the biggest hindrance for you in keeping a consistent prayer time?

2. Which part of your schedule is expendable? Where do you think you can make time for prayer?

3. What part of your day would be best for prayer? Are you a morning person or a night owl? How might that impact the time you choose to pray?

Action Steps

1. Next week, keep track of what you do during the day by logging your hourly activities. At the end of the week, see where you might be able to make room for a time of devotion.

2. Once you have found a time that works best for you, set your alarm as a reminder to pray. Commit to praying and having devotions at that time for two weeks straight or until it becomes a habit.

3. Sacrifice thirty minutes of television today, and use that time for prayer instead.

Once we have set aside time to pray, we struggle with what exactly we should be praying for. Do we have enough time to pray for everything and everyone on our lists? God tells us through His Word to pray for the mission of the Church (Matthew 9:38; Colossians 4:3), for the government (1 Timothy 2:2), for our brothers and sisters who are sinning (1 John 5:16), for those who are sick and suffering among us (James 5:13–16), for our church leaders (Hebrews 13:17–18), and the list goes on. I can imagine that we all pray for our family, friends, and neighbors. We pray for the military, for the oppressed and downtrodden, and for ourselves. This is probably only scratching the surface. The point is that there are so many things for which to pray, how can we keep track? Should we be praying for all of these things every day? If we try to cover all of these issues in one sitting, we will quickly burn ourselves out. It is important to go into our prayer time with a plan.

Imagine you are playing in an important football game against your extremely talented and strong archrivals. Winning this game is going to be hard, but victory would mean a trip to the Super Bowl. Now, imagine that on the Monday before the game the coach announces that this week you will not study the other team's strategy or practice any plays. Instead, you are just going to show up on Sunday and see what happens. How do you think your team would fare?

Alternatively, imagine you have been asked to perform in a dance recital in front of thousands of people. Your dance teacher is very excited and wants to see you do well. She presents you with a beautifully choreographed piece guaranteed to please the audience. But, as she is explaining the routine, you interrupt and let her know that once you get on stage, you are just going to wing it. How do you think your performance will turn out?

Now, apply these analogies to your prayer life. You have gone to church on Sunday and have set your alarm to have personal devotions starting this Monday. But when the alarm goes off, you kneel in a quiet place and realize you have nothing to say. Instead of thinking about what you will do with your time, you just sort of speak your mind. Your prayers have no direction and no aim. In fact, you find that you have a hard time staying focused or even awake! You leave your prayer time feeling like a football team with no strategy or a dancer with no routine. Everything seems scattered and chaotic.

A football team needs a game plan. A dancer needs choreography. A person of prayer needs focus. Without focus our prayer time can become aggravating. However, by implementing a game plan and choreographing our steps, we can bring order into chaos and have greater focus when we pray. This chapter will examine some practices that can assist us in focusing our faithful, regular time of prayer.

Structuring Your Time[1]

We all need patterns in our lives. God created the world in such a way that there was order. We are ordered creatures. The first chapter in Genesis is the story of God creating order against chaos. In the beginning, before God spoke, the Spirit was hovering over dark and tumultuous waters, but as soon as God started speaking, light overwhelmed the darkness. The waters were put under control as God separated them from the sky. Then, He created dry land so that the chaotic waters were not overwhelming everything. Chaos was undone by God's creative work (Genesis 1:1–13).

The way we worship, then, should be a reflection of the God we worship. Paul says as much to the Corinthians when he proclaims, "God is not a God of confusion but of peace" (1 Corinthians 14:33). Therefore, when we gather for worship, "all things should be done decently and in order" (v. 40). This is why every church service you attend has a liturgy of some kind. Liturgy means nothing more than intentional ordering of our time. Whether your worship service is considered contemporary or traditional, your time in that service is made up of a liturgy.

What is true of our corporate worship should be true of our personal prayer time as well. We all need a liturgy of some kind if we want to have a focused prayer time. Our time requires an ordering and pattern of some kind for us to function. The less order we have, the crazier our lives get. For example, what would happen if your job suddenly required you to work nights after years of working day shifts? Your life would be disoriented, and you would feel out of sorts until you got used to the new pattern. Having an ordered way of life is important for us to function efficiently.

Having a set pattern for our prayer helps us focus and stay on track. It prevents our minds from wandering aimlessly. Think of your personal prayer liturgy like a designed play for a football team and the elements of your prayer time like the players set to carry out the plays. You want the players to be in the right place and to know where they are headed. When everyone follows the designed play properly, the team's goals are reached more efficiently. Similarly, when you have each element in place, you know what you are going to say and why you are saying it. This way your mind doesn't wander off into your plans for the day.

To be sure, sometimes plays in a football game break down and the team has to adjust. A prayer-time liturgy is not a straightjacket you must wear. There will be times when you feel the need to pray for things that may not fit the order of things you typically follow, and some days you may feel like going with a different order because you do not want your prayer life to get too monotonous. That is all fine. The liturgy you work with is simply a tool to help keep you on task and focus your thoughts on Jesus. Here are some ways you can learn to structure your prayers.

FIND A DEVOTIONAL

It is not necessary for you to invent your own personal prayer liturgy. There is no shortage of devotional material designed to guide your time. You can find devotionals that will work for you no matter how much time and effort you are able to give to your personal prayer time. Let me offer three criteria you will want to follow when picking out a devotional:

1. **Biblically Based:** There are many devotionals that will seek to inspire you before they draw from the inspired Word! Make sure the devotional takes you through a significant portion of Scripture every day. It is helpful to use a devotional based on a book of the Bible so that you can pray your way through that book. If you find a thematic devotional, make sure the theme is biblical and not merely practical.

2. **Christ Centered:** Just because the devotional is biblically based does not mean that it will fix your eyes on Jesus. Many devotionals use the Word to direct us back on ourselves. They focus on us rather than Christ for us. The Scriptures are presented as a book of instructions rather than the story of salvation. Be sure Jesus is the hero of each devotion.

3. **Law-Gospel Balanced:** You may find a devotional that is biblically based and talks a lot about Jesus. However, it may still focus on me more than on what Jesus did and still does for me. When you are reading your devo-

tion, ask yourself these questions: Is this devotion only telling me to do something, or is it telling me what God has done for me in Christ? Is the emphasis here on instruction for the Christian or promises from Christ? It is not necessarily bad if there are instructions given; the Scriptures are full of laws and commands. But if all the devotion ever does is tell you how to live your life, it will only prove to suffocate the joy out of Christian living! Make sure the good news of what God has done for you in Jesus Christ dominates your devotional reading.

All three of these criteria are crucial. When I was in high school, I began reading through a very popular devotional. It was strong on the first and the second criteria. However, as I learned later, it was virtually void of the Gospel. I would read my devotion at night and lie awake terrified that because of my sinful day—because I had not, shall we say, given my utmost to God—He would not be pleased with me. I feared that I had lost my faith! A devotional that is void of the Gospel can be deadly. The Gospel must predominate. At the end of the chapter, in the "Action Steps" section, I will offer some suggestions for devotionals that meet these criteria.

PERSONAL PRAYER SERVICES

You may also consider using a hymnal at home. Not only does it contain the services we follow when we gather for worship, but it also contains some marvelous services for use in our personal prayer time. *Lutheran Service Book* (*LSB*), for example, provides a section for personal devotional use entitled "Daily Prayer for Individuals and Families" (pp. 294–98). Brief liturgies are provided for morning, noontime, early evening, or close of the day devotions. Sections of verses, or versicles, from the Psalms are provided for the appropriate part of the day. A song such as a hymn, canticle, psalm, or praise song can follow this. Readings are suggested, though if you are working through your own devotional reading, this would be a great time to meditate on the passages for that particular day. Next a reading from the catechism (or, again, whatever devotional you may be working through) is suggested. The Apostles' Creed is confessed. Then it is time for prayer.

The Lord's Prayer begins the prayers and is followed with whatever prayers you may have. *LSB* even offers daily prayer suggestions (p. 294). Many written prayers are provided to assist you in choosing what to pray for (pp. 305–18). Sometimes it is hard to find the words we want to use. These written prayers give voice to those things we are having a hard time saying. Finally, concluding prayers are offered to send us on our way in peace.

God hears our prayers whether we read them from someone else's pen or pray them from our own hearts. There is no need to speak condescendingly towards someone for how little or often they use written prayers.

You may also choose to work from one of the services found in the hymnal. As mentioned in the first chapter, corporate worship ought to give shape to our personal prayer time.

Using parts of the service from your congregation's worship service is one way you can keep your personal prayer time connected to the Divine Service. Learning parts from some of the other services—also known as prayer offices—will prove to be a fruitful exercise. The services of Matins, Vespers, Morning and Evening Prayer, and Compline all contain rich material for our prayers.

THE LITANY

Another option is to make the Litany a regular part of your personal prayer time (*LSB*, pp. 288–89). The Litany is an ancient form of prayer that seeks the Lord's favor for nearly all of the needs we face in this life. Like the personal prayer services, it can be prayed alone or in a group setting.

During the season of Lent, I have made it a practice to pray the Litany every day. It serves as a helpful topical outline for my prayers. For example, every Friday I pray for the Church at large and specifically for my brother pastors using a section of the Litany that looks like this:

L: To rule and govern Your holy Christian church; to preserve all pastors and ministers of Your Church in the true knowledge and understanding of Your wholesome Word and to sustain them in holy living;

To put an end to all schisms and causes of offense; to bring into the way of truth all who have erred and are deceived;

To beat down Satan under our feet; to send faithful laborers into Your harvest; and to accompany Your Word with Your grace and Spirit:

C: We implore you to hear us, good Lord.
(*LSB*, pp. 288–89)

Just before I implore God to hear this prayer, I bring my specific requests before Him. I pray for my brothers in the ministry by name, I pray for our church body and her leaders, and I pray for the Church throughout the world. This is one way of praying the Litany. However you pray this prayer, the Litany beautifully guides our prayers and requests.

Planning Ahead

Just as it is helpful to have your daily prayer time planned out, it is also helpful to know what you are going to be praying for ahead of time. Here are some ways you can prepare ahead of time for your prayers.

KEEPING TRACK

It is a good idea to develop a prayer list or a prayer journal. Lists and journals are beneficial for two reasons: First, they help us remember those things for which we want to pray. A missionary friend told me the heartbreaking story of a hospital call he once made. Along with some members from his church, he went to visit a former member who was very sick. After speaking with her and offering her words of encouragement, one of the men said, "We will pray for you." She replied, "Please don't say that. I used to be a Christian too. I used to say that. But I never really did it." As much as I want to hear this story and say, "Well, that was her problem!" I must confess my own sins. I too am guilty of saying "I will pray for you" with good intentions but then forgetting my commitment when I am sitting before the Lord. Carrying a small notepad to keep track of the things for which you want to pray is helpful for reminding you of your promises. You will also be ready to jot down a quick note every time something causes you to think, "Oh, I should pray for that!"

Second, a prayer journal is helpful for looking back on what we have prayed for and seeing how God has answered our prayers. Many people put great spiritual significance in keeping a prayer journal. I have never been one for journaling. However, I do see a great benefit in keeping track of prayers prayed. It can provide valuable content and context for our prayers. We may find answered prayers for which we want to give thanks. We may also find prayers that we may feel have not been answered. We can continue to lift them into the ears of our Father.

WEEKLY PRAYERS

Do not try to pray for everything on your list every day. You will burn out quickly. Instead, organize your daily prayers around different topics throughout the week. This way you will not feel overwhelmed by the number of people and situations you desire to lift before the Father. As mentioned earlier, *LSB* offers ideas of what you can pray for every day (p. 294).

Another option is to organize your week around the Lord's Prayer. For example, Sundays could be devoted to praying the First Petition, "Hallowed be Thy name." You could focus your prayer time on how God's name could be kept holy among you that day and throughout the week. You could pray for your church and your pastor, that as he preaches the Word, he would do so faithfully. Then, on Monday, you could focus your prayer time on the Second Petition and so on. With seven petitions this would be a pretty easy model to maintain.

Aside from not feeling like we have to pray for every issue every day, the great benefit of praying from a prepared list or structuring our week around the Lord's Prayer is that it prevents us from praying only about what is on our mind. It reminds us that prayer is about God, not about us. We are a part of a much larger world in a much larger story. Being reminded to pray, for example, for missionaries or the government pulls me out of my small corner and involves me in what God is doing throughout the world.

An example of a weekly prayer plan can be seen in the section on weekly prayers in *Lutheran Book of Prayer* (St. Louis: Concordia, 2005), beginning on page 14. Week 4 is built around the words and themes of the Lord's Prayer (p. 56).

Shut the Door: Preparing a Place

In the previous chapter, we examined the importance of finding time to pray. It is also important to find a good place to pray. Here we can learn from Jesus. After a long day of casting out demons, healing diseases, and feeding thousands of people with a few loaves of bread and a couple fish, Jesus sent His disciples away so He could be alone in prayer (Mark 6:45–46). Before He chose His twelve disciples, He went to a mountain to pray (Luke 6:12). He found places where He could be alone with His Father. He also tells us that when we pray, our only audience is God. So, instead of praying in places where others will be impressed by you, "go into your room and shut the door and pray to your Father who is in secret. And your Father who sees in secret will reward you" (Matthew 6:6).

It is important for our prayer time to be free from distractions. Thus, the best place to pray will be a place that allows you to focus on God and His Word. When I first became a pastor, I tried to have devotions in my office. I sat at my desk in front of the computer and attempted to focus my thoughts on God. This was a poor location since I was easily distracted. I had to fight the urge to turn the computer on, not to mention the fact that the piles on my desk only served to remind me of all I had to do that day. In an effort to fix the problem, I moved to another spot in my office. Focus still eluded me because my books and pictures caused my mind to wander. Finally, I moved into the sanctuary. Because the sanctuary is a place designated for worship, I found it to be the ideal location. It is free from distractions. The things that do catch my attention (such as the cross, the altar, the baptismal font, the seats of my brothers and sisters who need my prayers) serve to focus my prayers on Christ and His Church.

As a pastor, I am at an unfair advantage here as I work in a building designed for prayer. If you have daily access to your congregation's sanctuary, then that would be a wonderful place to pray. However, if that is inconvenient, it is best to find a place in your own home that is free from disturbances. In front of the television or computer is probably not the best place unless you are a very disciplined person. It is also probably a good idea to leave your cell phone in a different room. If you decide you want to pray at work, it may be harder to find a place free from distraction. However, if you can step away into your car or an empty office or find a nearby park, then you will be able to be alone with the Lord.

Strange as it sounds, it may be helpful to bring a cross or a crucifix with you to the place of prayer, but not so you can pray to it or through it in some idolatrous fashion. Rather, as you pray, it can serve to remind you of the Crucified One, who has opened the Father's ears to your prayers. It may draw your thoughts to your sins that nailed Christ to the cross and to the blood He shed to remove them. That great love and sacrifice not only make our prayers to God possible, but they are the very gifts prompting us to pray. Seeing a cross during my prayers serves to remind me of this marvelous truth, and it may do the same for you.

Not every place where one can be alone is ideal for extended prayer. Some people may feel that their drive to work is an ideal time for prayer. This may be a good time to be alone with our thoughts; however, driving a car demands our full attention. In prayer, we are to be focused on the Lord. As we drive, we are to be focused on our neighbor's vehicle. At such moments, deep prayer may distract us from our responsibility to not hit people with our car.

Make a habit of going to the same place at the same time every day. At first, you might struggle with distraction, but stick with it. Soon that place will become like a small sanctuary for you. Daily being in the same place at the same time will help focus your prayer time.

Praying with Your Whole Body

Another element to consider is how you will position your body when you pray. When I am struggling to find time to pray, I attempt to make up for it by praying in bed. What generally ends up happening is that I fall asleep while praying. Granted, it is not a bad way to fall asleep. However, my goal in praying is to be focused on God, not dozing off on Him! The position of my body in this situation is not conducive to meditating on God. How we position our bodies during our prayer has a major impact on our focus.

The Scriptures are full of examples of people praying with their whole body. We are creatures, body and soul. Thus, when we pray, our bodies and our souls work together. What we are doing physically reflects what we are experiencing spiritually. When the people of God are driven to repentance by God's Law or have cause for extreme angst, they often tear their clothes and cover themselves in sackcloth and ashes (Esther 4:1; Jonah 3:6–9). Since kneeling and bowing are signs of reverent submission, the psalmist calls for such actions as God's people enter His holy presence (Psalm 95:6). Hands are lifted up to God in both times of praise and times of despair (Psalm 134:2; Lamentations 3:40–41). There are even times when God's people should dance for joy over God's loving-kindness (Psalm 30:11; 149:3; 1 Chronicles 15:27–29). All of this demonstrates that how we position ourselves in prayer matters. The posture of our bodies is going to both reflect and impact what is going on in our spirits.

When I first heard this advice, I found it a little strange. I figured God heard my prayers whether I was lying in bed or lying prostrate on the ground. Of course the way we posture our bodies makes no impact on whether or not God hears our prayers. However, from our end of the conversation, the position of our bodies will impact our mindset. Some may choose to pray with their hands lifted up. Others may choose to fold their hands and bow their heads (an ideal position for children who are constantly tempted to fidget and play). I fold my hands and kneel while I pray because it puts me in a more reverent mindset. I am able to focus more on my prayers because I actually *feel* like I am praying! While no law commands that we fold our hands, bow our heads, or kneel, the position of our bodies will certainly impact the focus of our minds.

In order to stay focused during our prayer time, it is important for us to go in with a plan. Like a football team's playbook or a ballerina's choreographed routine, a personal prayer liturgy will help keep our minds fixed on Christ and His Word. By utilizing the resources provided by our church, such as the hymnal or other devotional material, we are able to organize our time in a rich and faithful manner. Thinking about where we pray and how we position ourselves will keep our minds set on the task at hand. These are just a few items to consider as we seek to organize our faithful, regular prayer time.

Key Points

- Having a plan will enable you to stay focused and on task.

- A personal prayer liturgy can guide your time of prayer.

- Finding a place free of distractions will help you focus on the Lord and His Word.

- A reverent and meaningful position will help you to stay focused during prayer.

Discussion Questions

1. Do you prefer to have order in your prayer time, or do you prefer things to be less structured? Why?

2. Have you ever used devotional material that frustrated

you? What was frustrating about it? Have you ever used devotional material that was a blessing to you? What made it that way?

3. What would the ideal place of prayer look like for you?

4. In what posture do you pray? Do you think changing your posture could impact your focus?

Action Steps

1. Use a devotional. You may want to ask your pastor which one he recommends. Here is a list of devotionals that I have found to be helpful:

   Portals of Prayer: These devotional booklets are a staple in most Missouri Synod congregations. Every day there are small devotions based on a reading from Scripture, as well as a prayer and a psalm suggestion. These are marvelous if you are just beginning to have devotions or if you have been doing devotions your whole life.

   Treasury of Daily Prayer (Concordia Publishing House, 2008): For my money this may be the most valuable and comprehensive devotional resource available. The readings are scheduled around the Church calendar. Every day you are provided with readings from the Psalms, the Old Testament, and the New Testament and a passage from some great theologian. A hymn verse and prayer are given at the end of the readings, followed by a suggested reading from the Book of Concord. In the middle of the book, worship services and personal prayer liturgies are provided for your use. There is much more, but this gives you a brief idea of this marvelous resource.

The Lord Will Answer: A Daily Prayer Catechism (Concordia Publishing House, 2004): This devotional is organized around the Church Year and Luther's Small Catechism. This is a great guide for praying through the catechism and is full of scriptural insights for daily living and challenging prayers and meditations from great theologians. To me it reads like a lighter version of the *Treasury of Daily Prayer.*

Through Faith Alone (St. Louis: Concordia, 1999): This little book provides daily meditations on Scripture and the Christian life from Martin Luther. This is a very insightful book, though I would recommend reading it alongside the Scriptures and using it as a part of your personal prayer liturgy.

I also recommend finding a Bible reading program that takes you through the Bible in one or two years. This is a great way of familiarizing yourself with the Scriptures without feeling overwhelmed by the amount of material contained in God's Word.

2. Make an effort to create a place where you will be able to focus on prayer.

3. Try praying in a different position this week to see if it helps you focus.

4. Begin to carry a small notepad with you to record prayer requests. Also, keep a journal of what you are praying for.

Prayer is a recognized practice by every world religion. But the difference between Christian and non-Christian prayers is as vast as the difference between salvation by faith and salvation by works. Non-Christian prayer seeks to get the god or gods on the side of the one praying. The goal is to manipulate, control, or appease the god(s) to work for you. Prayer arises out of fear or selfish desire. God is seen as nothing more than a stronger power that can fix our broken situations.

Christian prayer is radically different. We do not pray merely to get something out of God. We pray because of what we have already been given in Christ Jesus. We are not seeking to manipulate God in an effort to get Him to work for us. No, we pray to God because God has worked life and salvation for us. He has given us His own Son through whose shed blood our sins have been washed away (Romans 3:21–25). We have been adopted into His family through the Holy Spirit's work in the waters of Baptism (Galatians 3:27–4:7; Titus 3:4–7). Just like an adopted child, we have received a new name. We belong to the triune God, baptized in the name of the Father, Son, and Holy Spirit (Matthew 28:19). As the baptized, we pray confidently to God just as children speak to their loving father, because we know it is God's good pleasure to give us the Kingdom (Luke 12:32). We pray because of what we have already received.

Jesus has opened up the gates of heaven and poured out all of God's treasures upon us (Ephesians 3:16–19). The lines of communication between God and humans, which were closed off by sin, have been reopened through the sacrifice of Christ so that we are able to seek God's will and ask for His blessings, which He is all too ready to give (John 15:16; 16:26–27). Jesus says, "Ask, and it will be given to you; seek, and you will find; knock, and it will be opened to you. For everyone who asks receives, and the one who seeks finds, and to the one who knocks it will be opened" (Matthew 7:7–8).

It gets better. Not only does Jesus open up the communication lines between God and us, not only does He make incredible promises concerning God's response to our prayers, He takes it one step further and actually gives us prayers to pray! We do not have to go searching for the right mantra to chant or the key phrases that magically unlock secrets of heaven. God's Word is full of prayers that we have been given to say to God! God's Word not only invites us to pray, but it gives shape to our prayers and fills our hearts and mouths with the prayers themselves.

Praying with Open Bibles

Too often we view prayer as a means of escape from the world. We see it as a time to empty ourselves of all the stresses and anxieties that weigh us down. To be sure, prayer is a time to cast our cares upon Christ (Matthew 11:28–30). However, prayer is not a time to be emptied of all thought but to be filled by God's Word! While we cast our cares upon Christ, He freely gives us His gifts in return. Rather than leaving the world behind when we pray, we are actually seeking for the Lord to help us see the world from His perspective and to give us the strength we need to get through it. Praying with our Bibles open gives us that perspective.

We are to pray for God's will to be done in this world. When we read the Scriptures, we learn what His good and gracious will is. In this way, prayer can be viewed as a conversation with God. Too often, whether we would admit it or not, we expect God to speak to us in a mystical or extra-spiritual way. We pray for God to give us direction in our lives and then wait for a miraculous sign or a strong conviction. Though these things may come, they are not the primary way God speaks to us, nor are they all that reliable. Who is to say that burning feeling you get when awaiting an answer to prayer is not just indigestion? It is better to see that the conversation takes place through the Word, where the Holy Spirit is telling us what He thinks in a tangible way.

I know this may seem frustrating. It's especially hard when it comes to praying about big decisions in your life, like when deciding where to go to college or if it's a good time to move. There is no book of the Bible that has our specific life plan spelled out. God's will for my daily decisions is not found in Philippians, nor is there an "Epistle to Bob" in the canon. However, as we engage the Scriptures, we find God does have a great deal to say in answer to our prayers.

We want to know God's will for our future, thinking it will be some step-by-step outline of trials and accomplishments. Instead, we find that God's will is to forgive us for Christ's sake. His will is to be our Father whom we trust no matter what may come our way. God may not tell us specifically which college to choose, house to buy, or decision to make, but He does reveal to us that Christ has completely and fully turned away God's wrath from us (Romans 3:21–26; Hebrews 2:17). He promises us that by virtue of Baptism we are His children; therefore, there is no longer any condemnation for us (Romans 8:1). So, when we pray for wisdom in making a decision, we should do so knowing that God will not condemn or judge us for which choice we make. God answers our prayers by saying we are free to choose because we are making that choice as God's beloved child. His will is to love us no matter where we go! We can seek our Lord's will with confidence, knowing that His Word will give us guidance by always pointing us back to Christ.

Praying the Catechism

A catechism is nothing more than a book that teaches the core of the Christian faith. Thus it should come as no surprise that Luther's Small Catechism and Large Catechism offer brief summaries of the entire Christian life. Much like praying with an open Bible, praying these catechisms can guide our prayers as believers. From Luther's catechisms we learn God's will for our lives (the Law) in the Ten Commandments. We then learn who God is and what He has done for us (the Gospel) in the Apostles' Creed. These two words from God shape our prayers, which we learn to pray in the Lord's Prayer. Learning to pray our way through the catechism, then, is critical for learning to live the Christian life. Before we discuss how to pray the catechism, however, a few words should be said about the core prayer of the baptized: the Lord's Prayer.

THE LORD'S PRAYER

The disciples got it right for once. It was rare, but one of the disciples actually asked Jesus the right question. Usually, they would come to Jesus with questions about which of them was the greatest or who would get to have the best seat in God's kingdom. But, one day, as the disciples saw Jesus returning from a time of prayer, one of the Twelve approached Him and said, "Lord, teach us to pray" (Luke 11:1). This disciple was doing what disciples are supposed to do: he was seeking to learn from his Rabbi. He got it right! Jesus is our teacher when it comes to prayer.

Jesus responds to this request by giving the Church what we commonly call the Lord's Prayer. He gave the same prayer in the Sermon on the Mount when He said,

> Pray then like this: "Our Father in heaven,
> hallowed be Your name. Your kingdom come,
> Your will be done, on earth as it is in heaven.

Give us this day our daily bread, and forgive us our debts, as we also have forgiven our debtors. And lead us not into temptation, but deliver us from evil." (Matthew 6:9–13)

"There is no nobler prayer to be found upon earth than the Lord's Prayer. We pray it daily," said Luther (Large Catechism III 23). Here we have Christ not only commanding us to pray, but also giving us the very words that our Father delights to hear. This is a prayer we can pray with confidence, for God Himself has given it to us! All of the prayers in Scripture could be summarized with this one simple yet profound prayer.

This is not the place for us to delve into the depths of the profound theology contained in the Lord's Prayer. Martin Luther, among others, has done a masterful job of this in his catechisms (a necessary resource for anyone who wants to understand prayer in general and the Lord's Prayer specifically). However, a few observations will prove helpful as we learn to pray the prayer Jesus taught us.

As Luther said, we pray this prayer daily. Jesus wasn't merely offering us this prayer as one option among many. He said, "Pray then like this . . ." (Matthew 6:9). Emphasizing our Lord's instructions, Luther says, "[God] Himself arranges the words and form of prayer for us" (Large Catechism III 22). The Lord's Prayer is to be both the content of our prayer and the form or shape of our prayers.

A. The Content of Our Prayers

The Lord's Prayer is a precious gift given directly from heaven. It is a gift we are to use, to study, and to enjoy! It is to give shape to all of our prayers. Here Jesus has revealed to us the very thing our Father wants to hear. Trying to construct our own prayers apart from this gift would be like a father buying his son a new BMW for his birthday only to have the son leave the car in the garage because he would rather ride in the back seat of his buddy's Pinto. The father did not give his son that car to let it sit in the garage. He gave him that car so it would be driven! Christ did not give us the Lord's Prayer only for us to keep it in the garage until we feel like using it. Christ expects us to get a lot of mileage out of this prayer!

The Lord's Prayer is made up of seven petitions. These petitions can be separated into two categories: the "Thy" petitions and the "us" petitions. The "Thy" petitions consist of the following prayers: "Hallowed be Thy name," "Thy kingdom come," and "Thy will be done on earth as it is in heaven." These petitions place the focus of our prayers squarely on God and not on ourselves. We are so prone to dive into prayer by focusing only on our wants and desires, but as we have noted, prayer is about God and His will for us. In these petitions God alone is glorified. "Look, we have in these three petitions, in the simplest way, the needs that relate to God Himself. Yet they are all for our sakes" (Large Catechism III 68).

As we pray these petitions, we do so to a God who is most glorified in loving His children. So, when we pray that our Father's name be hallowed, we are praying that His already-holy name would be found holy among us. When we pray for His kingdom to come, we are praying that He would graciously make us a part of His kingdom (a prayer He has graciously answered by baptizing us in His name). We know God's will is going to be accomplished no matter what. But we simply pray in the Third Petition that it would be done in our lives as well. Because our own flesh, the world, and the devil constantly attack us and seek to drive us away from our Lord, this petition seeks for God's will to be done for us over and against these foes.

The second section is made up of the final four petitions and could be entitled the "us" petitions. After focusing our prayers on our Father who is in heaven, we now ask Him to give ear to our situations here on earth by asking Him to give us daily bread, forgive our sins, lead us not into temptation, and deliver us from evil. Though we are concerned with our needs in these four petitions, God's name is still glorified as we seek His help in our weakness. "Call upon Me in the day of trouble; I will deliver you, and you shall glorify Me" (Psalm 50:15).

In praying these petitions, we are doing nothing more than asking God to be who He is for us. When we ask for our daily bread, we are asking God to do the work of the Creator as "He richly and daily provides me with all that I need to support this body and life." (Small Catechism, First Article). When we pray for forgiveness for our trespasses, we are simply asking God to be the Redeemer who has "purchased and won me from all sins, from death, and from the power of the devil . . .with [Christ's] holy, precious blood and with [Christ's] innocent suffering and death" (Small Catechism, Second Article). And when we pray not to be led into temptation and to be delivered from evil, we are praying for the Father to send us His Holy Spirit so that we would not be found doing those things that are against His will. We are asking God to keep us in the Church with Jesus Christ and in the one true faith (Small Catechism, Third Article).

The "us" petitions keep us grounded in daily life. They remind us of our daily need for God. We pray from a position of helplessness. We glorify God when we call upon Him daily with the specific words He has given us to pray. Therefore, it is natural to find the Lord's Prayer on the lips of believers during personal prayer time. It is also good to pray it when we wake up and before we go to sleep, and these petitions become the primary content of our prayers.

B. The Form of Our Prayers

The Lord's Prayer, prayed just as Christ gave it to us, shapes the rest of our prayers. That is, the rest of our prayers fall under one of the seven petitions given to us by Christ. As we meditate upon and speak the prayer Christ gave us, we will find our thoughts directed towards those things in life that fall under each particular petition. For example, while praying the Third Petition ("Thy will be done"), we may find ourselves thinking about false teachers that arise around the Church. At such moments it would be appropriate to cry out to the Lord for deliverance and discernment. Or when facing a rough economy, we might be worried about where the next paycheck is coming from. Suddenly, our prayers for daily bread take on a new sense of urgency. God has provided us with the Lord's Prayer to give voice to whatever concerns may be weighing on our hearts.

When we are daily praying the Lord's Prayer, all of our other prayers will stem from it. We should not treat this prayer like a mantra that we mindlessly repeat into the air three times a day. Rather, by memorizing and repeating it, we allow it to renew our minds and form our prayers. As those who are baptized, we daily die to our old, sinful nature. The Lord's Prayer guides us in praying more faithfully as we seek to conform our prayers to God's will.

This may sound restrictive, as though I am saying God only likes the Lord's Prayer and will shut His ears to the rest—which is certainly not true. However, such thoughts fail to take into consideration the depths of the prayer Christ has bid us to pray. When we seek to conform our prayers to the Lord's Prayer, rather than seeing our prayer life more restricted, our prayers will become richer and deeper. The following model shows what this looks like practically.

A.C.T.S. Model for Praying the Catechism

Martin Luther had a barber named Peter who once asked him for advice on how he should pray. Luther responded with a letter entitled, "A Simple Way to Pray" (Matthew Harrison, trans. [St. Louis: Concordia, 2012]). In this letter he taught Peter to pray each part of the catechism using four points. In our day, Luther's "garland of four strands," as he calls it, has been tweaked just a bit and presented as the A.C.T.S. model. "A.C.T.S." stands for adoration, confession, thanksgiving, and supplication. Here is a closer look at what each word means:

Adoration is that time in prayer where we honor God's Word by focusing on what God is teaching us or promising to us at this point in the catechism. Our focus is neither on ourselves nor on what we can get from God. Rather, in adoration of God and His Word, we are being formed by what He has to say.

Confession is that time when, upon hearing what God has to say, we acknowledge our sinfulness to God. If we have been focusing on a commandment, we confess the ways in which we have broken that commandment. If we have been focusing on a promise, we confess our lack of faith in that promise. This is a time of self-examination and repentance.

Thanksgiving is when the sorrow of repentance is turned into rejoicing. Praying in faith means that we trust God to hear our cries and, because of Jesus' blood, to apply the promise of forgiveness to us. We thank Him for not holding our sins against us. We further thank Him for giving us this Word so that we can know Him better. If we are focusing on a command, we thank God for His wisdom and for the places where we see this command being fulfilled. If focusing on a promise, we thank God for His gifts, graciousness, and kindness towards sinners like us.

Supplication is when we close our prayers by asking God to help us do what He has commanded and believe what He has promised. Again, if focusing on a command, we pray that God will give us the abilities and resources necessary to obey His will. If we have been focusing on a promise, we pray that God will give us the faith to believe what He has decreed (for us!).

Luther suggested that each of these points be applied especially to the Lord's Prayer and the three articles of the Apostles' Creed. (Beyond this, it is certainly just as valuable to apply them to the Ten Commandments.) Here is an example of how it might look when praying the First Petition of the Lord's Prayer, "Hallowed be thy name":

Adoration: Father, Your name is truly holy above all other names. Though there are many enemies of Your name who would seek to usurp Your glory, they will all fail. You alone are almighty. At the name of Your almighty

Son, every knee will bow and every tongue will confess His lordship, to Your glory. Hear me now as I humbly pray to You in His name.

Confession: I confess that though Your name is truly holy, I have not always treated it as such. I have used Your name frivolously. I have cursed and sworn in Your name. I have lied to others and deceived them in Your name. I have appealed to other gods beside You. Worst of all, I have not trusted in Your name above all others. For the sake of Your dear Son's shed blood, forgive me for my sins. Have mercy on me for His name's sake!

Thanksgiving: I thank You, Father, that You have heard my prayer and have given Your Son to die for me. What is more, You have made me Your own by placing Your name on me when I was baptized. I thank You that you continue to reveal Yourself to me by name. I do not deserve such favor, but You are pleased to shower it upon me. For this I thank You, dear Father.

Supplication: For Jesus' sake, I ask now that Your name would be found holy in my life. May Your name be found on my lips in all times of trouble. Help me to give You praise and thanksgiving for all the good gifts You have bestowed upon me. Please give me boldness to proclaim Your name both into the ears of my fellow saints and into the ears of those who do not know You. Especially be with my dear friends who do not yet have faith. Put Your name on my lips so they may know of Your salvation. I ask all of this in Jesus' name. Amen.

These are not prayers you have to use. Certainly your prayers do not have to sound this formal. Your prayers should come from your heart. But you can see how praying in this way helps us to talk about God's Word with Him. He has spoken to us, and the A.C.T.S. outline allows us to engage with what He has said.

Engaging the Psalms

Though the Lord's Prayer is the fundamental prayer we find in the Scriptures, it is not the only prayer. God has given us a whole book of prayers in the Psalms. We might think of each psalm as an expansion of the Lord's Prayer since each finds a home under one of its petitions. To go deeper into praying the Lord's Prayer, then, it is important for us to pray the Psalms.

Our Lord Himself prayed the Psalms. More than this, He fulfilled what they said! He taught us how they spoke of Him (Mark 12:36; Luke 24:44). Time and time again the apostles demonstrated how the Psalms were pointing to Jesus (Acts 2:25–28; 4:25–26; Hebrews 1:5, 8–13; 2:6–8). Christ Himself even prayed a psalm of lament as He cried from the cross, "My God, My God, why have You forsaken Me?" (Matthew 27:46). When we pray the Psalms, we are praying about Christ with the very prayers our Lord Himself prayed.

Too often we approach the Psalms academically.[1] We

wonder what the context was for this particular prayer. We ask: Who wrote this psalm? When did the people of Israel pray it? How might I categorize this particular psalm? Though these and other interpretive questions are important to ask when studying the Psalms, this section of God's Word is primarily given to us as a prayer book. These are words God has given us to pray. Rather than merely studying their historical context, we want to interact with them in a more personal way.

Think of meditating upon the Psalms like getting to know new friends. As you engage them in conversation, you seek to understand their thoughts, their feelings, their struggles, and their joys in an effort to know how better to interact with them. You will often seek to identify with them by trying to draw connections between their life experiences and your own. So it is with the Psalms.

When a psalm is crying out in praise, seek to find out why. Ask yourself where in your own life God has given you cause to sing such a jubilant song. When you encounter a psalm of lament, rather than try and avoid the harsh language or find a theological way out of it, ask yourself when you have felt the same frustrations toward God or the world. Then, sit in awe of a God who gives you words to voice your frustrations toward Him! Remember, though they offer us some of the richest theology in all of Scripture, the Psalms are not theological treatises. They are sincere prayers of faith spoken honestly to our Father in heaven.

By praying the Psalms, we actually learn to pray more prayers than our own hearts could ever have imagined. No matter what you are going through, there is a psalm for you to pray. Here we learn to give voice to our joys and sorrows, our frustrations and our confusions, our anger and our pleasure. We will even find prayers that we are not sure we can pray without offending God. And yet, He is the one who has given us this book to pray!

Memorizing and praying the Psalms will result in a fuller, richer prayer life. My personal practice is to get to know one psalm a week. I pray it every day, whether that psalm fits my current situation or not. By praying psalms that do not fit my current attitude, I am reminded that the Psalms are bigger than me and that prayer is about God's will being done. Further, this practice helps me familiarize myself with all the psalms so that when I want to pray a prayer of lament or praise, I know where to turn.

An aid in praying is *Reading the Psalms with Luther* (St. Louis: Concordia, 2007). Each psalm is prefaced by a summary that helps put the psalm in a context. After the psalm, a short prayer is provided that can be used as a prayer starter.

God has not left us to figure out prayer on our own. Rather, He who has commanded us to pray has provided us with the prayers He wants to hear. He gives us the Lord's Prayer and the Psalms. Not only are they to be the content of our prayers, but they give shape to the way we pray as we seek to live out our faith. The Holy Spirit provides answers to our prayers and guidance to our lives as we turn to His inspired Word, which is a lamp to our feet and a light to our path (Psalm 119:105). As we pray, may God's Word be found in our hearts, in our minds, and on our lips.

Key Points

- Through the Word of God, the Holy Spirit not only invites you to pray, but gives you the prayers your Father wants to hear.

- You should consider praying with an open Bible. Your prayer time is a time to be filled up by God's Word.

- You should consider praying the Lord's Prayer daily along with the rest of the catechism (i.e., the Ten Commandments and the Apostles' Creed).

- Getting to know the Psalms will enrich and deepen your prayer life.

Discussion Questions

1. Are you used to praying the words of Scripture? Are you comfortable doing so?

2. How do you feel about praying psalms that call for God's judgment? How do think we should understand such prayers in light of Jesus' instructions to "love your enemies and pray for those who persecute you" (Matthew 5:44)? Where is God's judgment on all sin seen most clearly?

3. What do you think of the A.C.T.S. prayer model? Do you know of any other models that are helpful?

Action Steps

1. As you pray, think about the Lord's Prayer. Ask yourself under which petition your prayers could be categorized. Imagine in what situations Jesus found Himself when He may have prayed that same petition. For example, when would Jesus have sought deliverance in the face of temptation? Or when might Jesus have prayed for daily bread?

2. Begin to use the A.C.T.S. prayer model as you pray your way through the catechism. Start tomorrow with the First Commandment. Read the commandment and explanation. Let those words guide your prayers.

3. Begin to pray one psalm a day or to memorize one psalm at a time. As you do, ask yourself the following questions:

   a. When might Jesus have prayed this prayer? How does this help me understand Him better?

   b. Under which petition of the Lord's Prayer would this fit and why?

   c. How does this psalm make me feel? Am I comfortable praying these words or not? Why? What would drive the psalmist to pray this way? Can I identify with that?

d. Where does this psalm fit into what I am going through or have experienced in the past? In the same way, how does it apply to others I know? How could I pray it for them?

4. As you pray and study the Scriptures, use your prayer journal to record meaningful verses or sections of Scripture that show how God has answered your prayers.

The great saints of old who were considered men and women of prayer always amaze me. Waking before sunrise, they prayed for hours before ever entering the business of their day. Their minds were so saturated with love for God that they carried on conversations with Him throughout the day as if He were standing right in front of them. Their time of prayer was filled with tears and great affections. They even felt that without this daily encounter with God in prayer they would die for lack of spiritual sustenance. I am in awe of saints like Paul who, perhaps while praying, was carried into the third heaven (2 Corinthians 12:1–5), not to mention the psalms of David, which amaze me with their mixture of honest struggle and beautiful poetry. Prayer for these people seems so natural, so phenomenal, so spiritual.

I, on the other hand, fall asleep during my prayers. I hit the snooze button when the alarm goes off. When I actually sit down to pray, my mind wanders in five different directions. Sometimes I feel excellent after praying, while at other times I feel like I merely went through the motions. I know it is necessary to pray, but it is not natural for me. Afterwards, I do not always feel spiritually charged. While I am in awe of the great saints of prayer, I am not one of them. I feel more like the sleepy disciples in the Garden of Gethsemane before Christ's betrayal. "The spirit indeed is willing, but the flesh is weak" (Mark 14:38). I begin to wonder if something is wrong with me or if my faith is not as strong as it should be.

Perhaps you are one of the great saints of prayer. If so, praise God for this priceless gift! But perhaps you are more like me, wondering if your struggles mean there is something wrong with you. If that is the case, let me let you in on a little secret (which is neither small nor hidden): There *is* something wrong with us. We are sinners. Prayer is a struggle for us because we are constantly battling with the devil, the world, and our own sinful flesh! If our faith were perfect, our prayer life would have no hiccups. But our faith wavers like the waves in the sea so that our prayer life is sporadic.

The good news is that our confidence in prayer does not depend upon the strength of our faith. Rather, our confidence is in the almighty and merciful God who hears our prayers for the sake of His Son. Since Christ has removed the shackles of sin, He has freed us to prayerfully approach our heavenly Father. The difficulty is learning to get used to this freedom. Likely this is because we fail to grasp just what a miraculous gift has been granted to us in prayer. Since we are free, we are allowed to struggle with maintaining a faithful, regular prayer life—and we will. But we strive to pray nonetheless. As we strive and struggle, there are dangers we want to avoid, lest we give up altogether. Our goal is to achieve consistency in our prayer life, not to lose heart. In this final chapter, we will examine dangers we may run into in seeking a faithful regular prayer life and how we can find strength amidst our struggle from the very God who has invited us to pray.

Three Dangers

Here are three dangers that we want to be aware of as we seek to establish our prayer time:

Danger #1: GREAT EXPECTATIONS

The first danger we want to avoid is having too high of expectations for ourselves. As self-defeating as this initially may sound, we must establish our prayer life with a healthy level of honesty. After reading this book, you will not be a prayer expert. Your struggles will not go away. If you expect to set your alarm for tomorrow's first morning prayer time and never struggle again, you are in for a big disappointment.

No one ever becomes good at anything without working at it. Basketball players do not start making free throws without practicing for hours at a time. Musicians do not sit down and compose symphonies without first learning how to read and hear music. Christians who seek to have a faithful, regular prayer life do not just wake up one day and have angelic experiences. It takes time. You are going to have to discipline yourself to keep up with your prayer schedule. You are going to have to work at memorizing psalms, fight against mindlessly reciting the Lord's Prayer, and experiment with different liturgical formats until you find one that suits you. Being comfortable in a faithful and regular prayer time will come. It just won't come tomorrow.

In this vein, I want to revisit something touched on at the beginning of this chapter. It's tempting to read about the great heroes of the faith and try to emulate their prayer lives. To be sure, it's healthy to learn from those who seem to have a grasp on prayer. However, be cautious. In almost all cases, their "expertise" came with a large amount of struggle. What is more, many of them would not consider themselves experts on prayer at all. Rather, as with the rest of us, they probably felt as if they were struggling to pray as much as they would like.

Set achievable goals for yourself. If you do not already have a faithful, regular prayer time, do not begin by trying to fill up two full hours. Start small. Perhaps you can set aside fifteen or twenty minutes to read a psalm, work through a short devotion, and pray the Lord's Prayer. Once this becomes a pattern, you can add more time and elements to your personal prayer time.

Danger #2: PUTTING OFF TILL TOMORROW WHAT MUST BE DONE TODAY

There is always the danger of postponing prayer. Like the person who repeatedly announces that his or her diet will begin tomorrow, we often desire to make time for prayer but let too many other things get in the way. I could throw a lot of clichés at you right now: "There is no time like the present!" "Why put off till tomorrow what you can do today?" "Why wait? Call now!" However, those would make this danger seem petty. The reality is that you do not have a good reason to put off prayer any longer. In fact, you have the greatest reason in the world to start praying right now: God commands prayer!

Luther speaks strongly on this point when he warns, "So here prayer is not left to my will to do it or leave it undone, but it shall and must be offered at the risk of God's wrath and displeasure" (Large Catechism III 9). This may seem harsh, but we are masters at finding excuses. This kind of straight talk is necessary if we are to shoot down any excuse we may come up with for putting off prayer.

Though it is hard for us to recognize this as relatively wealthy Americans, our needs are vast. The fact that we cannot immediately recognize our needs is itself a reason to run to Christ for a great dose of perspective! The devil, the world, and our own flesh are constantly attacking us. We sing of this reality in the hymn "I Walk in Danger All the Way":

> I walk in danger all the way.
> The thought shall never leave me
> That Satan, who has marked his prey,
> Is plotting to deceive me.
> This foe with hidden snares
> May seize me unawares
> If I should fail to watch and pray.
> I walk in danger all the way. (*LSB* 716:1)

Given this reality, putting off prayer is like the man who notices a sharp pain in his shoulder and does his best to ignore it. Though his wife urges him to go to the doctor, he refuses. The longer he puts it off, the more painful it becomes, until it finally results in a heart attack. The longer we put off going to our Lord in prayer, the more likely we are to fall into temptation and be overwhelmed by the world.

There is no time to waste! If you are the diet-starts-tomorrow kind of person, then put the book down and start praying now! If you do not need to act that quickly, then before you go to bed tonight plan out your prayer time for tomorrow. Whatever excuses you are thinking right now need to be silenced. There is no excuse to not pray immediately.

Danger #3: GIVING UP

Working toward a faithful, regular prayer life can feel like joining a gym for a New Year's resolution—you are really fired up to begin! You buy the latest workout manual guaranteed to make your body look amazing in ninety days. At first, you are working out three times a week and are doing really well. But in February something comes up that interrupts your flow. Suddenly, you're finding excuses to stay home. Your routine starts to seem monotonous and you get bored. You stick with it until March, but by then you are struggling to work out even once every other week. At the end of the month, you find yourself on the phone making up some story to get out of your membership contract! When New Year's Eve rolls around the next year, you completely abandon resolutions because you think, "What's the point if I'm only going to fail?"

This is a danger when reading a book like this on prayer. You find some good ideas to work with, you set your time and place, you get an inspiring and theologically sound devotional, and you begin. Things go well for about a month and then, well, you know the rest of the story.

To be honest, this may happen. But, the right reaction is not to quit saying, "What's the point?" Life ebbs and flows. There will be times of great devotional success, and there will be times when the excuses to sleep in win out. But this is not failure, at least not yet. The only way you can fail at having a faithful, regular prayer life is to not try.

To encourage us, Jesus once told a parable on being persistent in prayer (Luke 18:1–8). Luke introduces the account by saying, "And he told them a parable to the effect that they ought always to pray and not lose heart" (v. 1). Jesus told the story of a widow who sought justice against her adversaries by constantly badgering a godless judge. Though he cared nothing for the widow and her cause, the judge grew tired of her constant requests and granted her justice. If this is how an unrighteous judge acts toward this woman in need, how much more lovingly will our Father in heaven "give justice to His elect, who cry to Him day and night" (v. 7)? With this parable Jesus lovingly shows us that He does not want us to grow weary and lose heart in our prayers, especially in the face of difficulties. He reminds us of the Father's great love for His children and His willingness to hear and answer them. "I tell you, He will give justice to them speedily" (v. 8).

Don't give up just because you are struggling to sustain a faithful, regular prayer life. Fight through the struggles. If the time you have chosen is not working, change times. If the devotional is not catching your interest, find a new one. If your personal prayer liturgy is getting monotonous, change it up with a different service. If you are falling asleep, drink coffee. But, whatever you do, do not stop fighting for a faithful, regular prayer time. There is too much at stake! Seeking to devour you, the devil is just waiting to pounce. This world's allurements are always trying to draw us back into the darkness away from Christ's marvelous light. We certainly cannot trust ourselves against such enemies since our old sinful nature continues to fight against us too. To have a faithful, regular prayer time is to wage war against these adversaries. It is a cry for help to our victorious Lord from the spiritual battlefield. He who has crushed the devil's head, overcome the world, and in Baptism crucified our sinful, weak flesh fights for us! And He is listening! The promise of answered prayer in the midst of our struggles is reason enough to fight for a faithful, regular prayer time.

Key Points

- You should not beat yourself up over the fact that you struggle to have a faithful and regular prayer life, but the struggle should not stop you from trying.

- Do not try to become an expert at prayer right away.

- Since you are constantly under attack, it is critical that you fight for a faithful, regular prayer life.

Discussion Questions

1. Do you find yourself feeling upset over your prayer life? How do you typically react? Do you give up or try harder? What steps can you take to overcome your frustrations?

2. Which of the three dangers listed above is most problematic for you? Why?

3. Are there other dangers you have encountered when trying to establish a faithful and regular prayer life? How have you dealt with them?

4. What comfort do you draw from Christ's promise that our God will faithfully answer your prayers?

Action Steps

1. Before the week is over, pick three action steps from previous chapters and implement them in your prayer life.

2. Before the day is over, set a time to pray tomorrow. Also, begin to look for a devotional you can use.

3. Pray right now! Give God thanks for the gift of prayer. Ask Him to guide you into a richer and deeper faithful and regular prayer life!

The Power of a Listening God

God has given us prayer as a gift, and He wants us to use it. Christ graciously invites us to pray directly to our Father and empowers us to do so by giving us the Holy Spirit. He says, "Truly, truly, I say to you, whatever you ask of the Father in My name, He will give it to you. . . . Ask, and you will receive, that your joy may be full" (John 16:23–34). We can pray to the Father because we belong to Christ. We have a God who listens and graciously answers His children. Both this invitation and this promise enable us to pray.

YOU CAN PRAY BECAUSE GOD INVITES YOU TO

Christ's invitation to pray is not a joke. Prayer is not some generic spiritual exercise that comes highly recommended from theologians and spiritual gurus everywhere. No, this is a serious command from Christ. God's name is hallowed when we pray. That is to say, when we pray, we are obeying the Second Commandment, "You shall not take the name of the LORD your God in vain" (Exodus 20:7). To fulfill this commandment is to "call upon [His name] in every trouble, pray, praise, and give thanks" (Small Catechism, Second Commandment). So, Luther says, "We are required to praise that holy name and call upon it in every need, or to pray. To call upon God's name is nothing other than to pray [e.g., 1 Kings 18:24]" (Large Catechism III 5). We must pray because God commands us to pray.

Imagine you are lost in the desert and have not had any food or water in days. Your life is hanging by a thread. As you are wandering hopelessly, you hear the sound of a helicopter in the distance. Suddenly, above your head you see the chopper with a man repelling down to grab you and pull you up. He says to you, "You must take my hand, I'll lift you to safety where we have food and water." You will grasp that hand with what little might you have. His command was an invitation to receive what you needed most in that moment. So it is with the command to pray. Again, Luther says,

> For by this commandment God lets us plainly understand that He will not cast us away from Him or chase us away [Romans 11:1]. This is true even though we are sinners. But instead He draws us to Himself [John 6:44], so that we might humble ourselves before Him [1 Peter 5:6], bewail this misery and plight of ours, and pray for grace and help [Psalm 69:13]. (Large Catechism III 11)

The command to pray is a law to which God has graciously attached a promise. We can pray with certainty, knowing that it is our gracious heavenly Father who beckons us to ask Him for help. These are not the demands of some self-concerned deity who must be persuaded to help us. Prayer is nothing more than children asking their Father to share His love. Our Father wants us to seek Him, "praying at all times in the Spirit, with all prayer and supplication" (Ephesians 6:18).

When we do this, He promises to answer. It is just as our Lord taught us,

> Or which one of you, if his son asks him for bread, will give him a stone? Or if he asks for a fish, will give him a serpent? If you then, who are evil, know how to give good gifts to your children, how much more will your Father who is in heaven give good things to those who ask Him! (Matthew 7:9–11)

It is to that promise that we now turn.

YOU CAN PRAY BECAUSE GOD PROMISES AN ANSWER

God graciously answers our prayers. We can never over-emphasize that word "graciously." Our Father listens to and answers our prayers because of His willingness to do it, not because of any sort of worthiness in us. He does not owe us answered prayers, but He lovingly gives good answers of His own volition. This is wonderful news! This means that we do not have to worry about the strength or sincerity of our prayers. The answer to our prayer lies in the heart of God, not in the worth of my half-heartfelt cries.

It is very popular to talk about the power we possess when we pray. You will hear about the power of a praying church or city or spouse. The idea is that our prayers carry a power to influence the world. In these circumstances, James is often quoted when he says, "The prayer of a righteous person has great power as it is working" (5:16). The assumption is that if we want to make a real impact in this world, then it is up to us to exercise the power of prayer.

But James is not exalting in the power inherent in a praying Christian or even in the prayer itself. Rather, he is pointing us to the fact that prayer is an appeal to God for help. Prayer does not contain power in and of itself. God is all-powerful. He gives us prayer as a way of turning to Him in our helplessness. The prayers of a righteous person are powerful, as James says, only because the One they appeal to has all power, glory, honor, and might! The Almighty is graciously inviting us to appeal to Him for help that He alone can give. Our hope is secure, not in the power of the praying person, but in the God who listens!

We can pray with confidence because God Himself prays for us and with us. Christ, our Brother and High Priest, has reconciled us to God through His blood. He now lives to intercede for us. That is another way of saying that Jesus loves to pray to God on our behalf (Hebrews 7:25). We pray in the name of Christ and with Christ! What is more, Christ has sent us the Holy Spirit to guide us into all truth (John 16:13). When we were baptized, we were adopted into God's family and we received the Holy Spirit. As Romans 8:15 says, "You have received the Spirit of adoption as sons, by whom we cry, 'Abba! Father!'" We can pray because we have the Holy Spirit who drives us to do it. What is more, in one of the most stunning promises concerning prayer ever uttered, Paul says,

Likewise the Spirit helps us in our weakness. For we do not know what to pray for as we ought, but the Spirit Himself intercedes for us with groanings too deep for words. And He who searches hearts knows what is the mind of the Spirit, because the Spirit intercedes for the saints according to the will of God. (Romans 8:26–27)

What does this all mean? It means that you can have a faithful and regular prayer life because God has given you prayer as a gift. Christ and the Holy Spirit are joining you in your prayers and interceding on your behalf. God answers your prayers because He is gracious, not because we deserve it or have to earn it. Even though we do not know how to pray, the Holy Spirit intercedes for the baptized according to God's will. The Holy Spirit is praying for you. Jesus, your great High Priest, whose blood has opened to us the kingdom of heaven, is praying for you. And God your Father is listening!

Chapter 3

1. I am indebted to William Cwirla's presentation, "Diets and Devotions: Can You Have a Devotional Life If You Are Neither a Mystic or a Pietist?" presented at the 2012 Pacific Southwest District's Pastor's Conference.

Chapter 4

1. For many of the insights on reading the Psalms, I am indebted to Dr. Timothy Saleska and his presentations at the 2012 Pastor's Conference for the Pacific Southwest District of the LCMS.